LOST CIVILIZATIONS

Lost Civilizations

EXPLORING THE WORLD'S FORGOTTEN EMPIRES

B. Vincent

QuantumQuill Press

Contents

1

Chapter 1: Introduction to Lost Civilizations

Definition and Importance

In the tremendous territory of mankind's set of experiences, certain human advancements have blurred into a lack of definition, abandoning baffling hints of their reality. These lost civic establishments, covered in the fogs of time, hold significant importance in disentangling the embroidery of our common past. In any case, what precisely characterizes lost progress, and for what reason would it be a good idea for us to give our academic undertakings to their review?

A lost development, in its essence, alludes to a once-prosperous society that has disappeared from the chronicles of history, abandoning the meager remainders of its presence. These confounding societies, frequently clouded by the ways of the world or gulped by the profundities of the earth, offer tempting looks into the intricacies of old human social orders. By diving into the secrets of these failed-to-remember domains, we set out on an excursion to recreate the story of human progress, sorting out parts of the past to enlighten the pathways of our aggregate legacy.

The investigation of lost developments isn't just a scholarly pursuit; it is a journey to grasp the complexities of human social development.

These disappeared social orders, with their one-of-a kind traditions, innovations, and conviction frameworks, offer significant bits of knowledge into the variety of human experience and the powers that shape the ascent and fall of civic establishments. Through their investigation, we gain a more profound comprehension of the flexibility and delicacy of human social orders, as well as the getting-through heritages that rise above the progression of time.

In addition, the meaning of concentrating on lost developments stretches beyond simple scholastic interest, conveying significant ramifications for contemporary social orders. By analyzing the victories and afflictions of antiquated developments, we gather significant illustrations that resound with our advanced difficulties. Whether it be ecological manageability, social disparity, or international flimsiness, the reverberations of past developments resonate through the passageways of time, offering wake-up calls and rousing stories that illuminate our present-day attempts.

Fundamentally, the investigation of lost civic establishments fills in as an extension between the past and the present, enlightening the interconnectedness of mankind's set of experiences and motivating us to chart a course towards a more illuminated future. As we leave on this scholarly odyssey to unwind the secrets of failed-to-remember domains, let us regard the call to dive further into the chronicles of history, for in those lie the keys to opening the mysteries of our common mankind.

Difficulties and Restrictions

The quest for understanding lost civilizations isn't without its difficulties and restrictions. As we try to uncover the privileged insights of old social orders, we are faced with a heap of impediments that block our journey for information. From the shortage of archeological proof to the innate predispositions of verifiable records, exploring the intricacies of concentrating on lost civilizations requires a nuanced comprehension of the impediments that lie in our way.

One of the essential difficulties in concentrating on lost civic establishments originates from the fragmentary idea of the archeological record. Centuries of disintegration, cataclysmic events, and human mediation have darkened a considerable number of the substantial remainders of old social orders, abandoning just tempting pieces of their reality. Archeologists and specialists should battle with inadequate curiosities, divided engravings, and subtle remnants, sorting out the riddle of the past with fastidious consideration and tender, loving care.

Besides, the translation of archeological proof is frequently laden with uncertainty and subjectivity. As scientists wrestle with unraveling old texts, recreating antiquated scenes, and deciphering social curiosities, they should explore the intricacies of inclination, bias, and hypothesis. The intrinsic limits of our comprehension, combined with the assorted viewpoints of researchers from various disciplines, can prompt disparate translations and clashing hypotheses about the idea of lost developments.

Notwithstanding the difficulties presented by the archeological record, specialists should likewise fight with the predispositions and restrictions of verifiable sources. Composed records of old civilizations, while priceless in giving experiences into their social practices and political designs, are much of the time shaded by the viewpoints of the creators and the plans of their peers. Isolating reality from fiction, knowing truth from fantasy, and contextualizing verifiable records inside their socio-political setting require a nuanced approach that recognizes the intricacies of human memory and story development.

Moreover, the investigation of lost developments is frustrated by the innate impediments of our advanced philosophies and innovations. While advances in archeological strategies, remote-detecting innovation, and interdisciplinary cooperation have extended our ability to uncover the mysteries of the past, we are still limited by the limitations of our contemporary apparatuses and methods. As we peer into the profundities of history, we should stay insightful about the inborn predispositions and restrictions that shape how we might interpret antiquated human advancements.

In spite of these difficulties and restrictions, the quest for understanding lost civilizations remains a commendable undertaking, offering significant bits of knowledge into the intricacies of mankind's set of experiences and social development. By recognizing the deterrents that lie in our way and moving toward our exploration with modesty and interest, we can expect to disentangle the secrets of failed-to-remember domains and enlighten the pathways of our common past.

Degree and Outline

In digging into the domain of lost human advancements, portraying the extension and broadness of our exploration is basic. The material of mankind's set of experiences is immense and varied, including a huge number of old societies and civic establishments that have risen and fallen over centuries. In this section, we leave on an excursion that traverses landmasses and ages, crossing the scenes of days past to uncover the leftovers of civilizations lost to time.

The civic establishments canvassed in this book address a different cluster of societies and social orders that once flourished during this phase of history. From the ripe fields of Mesopotamia to the thick wildernesses of Mesoamerica, every civilization offers a one-of-a kind window into the intricacies of old human social orders and the powers that molded their ascent and fall. By inspecting the accomplishments, developments, and traditions of these failed-to-remember realms, we gain a more profound appreciation for the rich embroidery of human progress and the getting-through engraving of our predecessors upon the world.

Our investigation will encompass a large number of developments from various geological locales and verifiable periods. From the mysterious Indus Valley Civilization to the superb Maya Domain, we will navigate the globe looking for pieces of information and unwinding the secrets of lost civic establishments. Every part will give a far-reaching outline of a particular development or gathering of civilizations, diving into their beginnings, accomplishments, decline, and getting through inheritances.

Besides, our investigation will stretch beyond the domains of archaic exploration and history to encompass interdisciplinary points of view and approaches. By drawing upon bits of knowledge from the humanities, etymology, natural science, and different fields of study, we desire to acquire a more all-encompassing comprehension of the powers that formed the directions of old civilizations. Through this multidisciplinary approach, we intend to reveal new insight into old secrets and uncover the secret insights of lost civilizations.

As we leave on this scholarly odyssey through the archives of history, let us remember the significance of setting, point of view, and lowliness in our quest for information. The investigation of lost civic establishments isn't simply a scholastic activity; it is a journey of disclosure that provokes us to defy our biases, extend our points of view, and develop a more profound appreciation for the intricacies of human experience. Together, let us venture into the core of ancient history to uncover the privileged insights of failed-to-remember domains and enlighten the pathways of our common past.

Strategies and approaches

The investigation of lost developments requires a complex methodology that draws upon a different exhibit of philosophies and disciplines. As we try to unwind the secrets of old social orders, we should utilize a blend of archeological uncovering, verifiable examination, logical examination, and near study to sort out the riddle of the past.

Prehistoric studies fill in as the foundation of our investigation, providing substantial proof of antiquated developments through the exhumation of material remaining parts. Through careful uncovering and examination of antiques, designs, and human remaining parts, archeologists can remake the material culture and lifeways of lost civic establishments, revealing insight into their day-to-day schedules, social designs, and mechanical accomplishments.

Notwithstanding paleo history, verifiable examination assumes a vital role in how we might interpret lost civic establishments. By investigating put-down accounts, engravings, and antiquated texts, antiquarians can gather experiences into the political, social, and strict elements of old social orders, giving significant setting to deciphering archeological discoveries and recreating authentic stories.

Moreover, the investigation of lost civic establishments benefits from interdisciplinary cooperation, drawing upon experiences from fields like the humanities, phonetics, natural science, and hereditary qualities. Anthropological examinations offer insights into the social practices and conviction frameworks of old social orders, while phonetic investigation can reveal insight into antiquated dialects and correspondence organizations. Ecological science gives important information on climatic circumstances, normal assets, and natural change, which can help contextualize the ascent and fall of civilizations. Likewise, hereditary investigations offer bits of knowledge into populace developments, hereditary variety, and natural variations, giving important insights into the starting points and relocations of old people groups.

Besides, relative examination assumes a significant part in our investigation of lost civic establishments, permitting us to draw equals and differences between various social orders and societies. By looking at likenesses and contrasts in engineering, craftsmanship, innovation, and social association, specialists can acquire a more profound comprehension of the social elements and cooperations that formed the improvement of old civilizations.

In utilizing these strategies and approaches, it is fundamental to stay aware of the limits and predispositions intrinsic to our wellsprings of proof. The investigation of lost developments is a complicated and iterative interaction, expecting researchers to assess and decipher the accessible information with thoroughness and suspicion. By embracing a multidisciplinary approach and encouraging open exchange and cooperation, we can expect to disentangle the secrets of old social orders and gain a more extravagant comprehension of the human experience across reality.

Setting the stage

Prior to diving into the nitty-gritty assessment of individual lost civic establishments, making way for our excursion into the profundities of antiquity is basic. This section fills in as a preface to the rich embroidery of history that we are going to disentangle, giving a fundamental setting and outlining our investigation inside the more extensive story of human progress.

We start by following the beginnings of development itself, investigating the rise of intricate social orders and the change from agrarian ways of life to settled farming networks. From the prolific valleys of the Tigris and Euphrates to the banks of the Nile and the Indus, we uncover the early groundworks of human development and the seeds of advancement and social trade that would shape the course of history.

As we progress through the sections, we will experience a different exhibit of lost civic establishments, each with its own remarkable story to tell. From the fantastic accomplishments of Mesopotamia to the mysterious vestiges of the Indus Valley, from the transcending pyramids of Egypt to the mind-boggling city-territories of Mesoamerica, we will cross continents and ages to reveal the insider facts of old social orders lost to time.

In any case, our process doesn't end with the investigation of individual civilizations. En route, we will likewise dig into more extensive topics and questions that rise above individual societies, like the idea of force and authority, the elements of exchange and trade, and the effect of natural change on human social orders. By contextualizing our investigation within these more extensive subjects, we desire to acquire a more profound comprehension of the interconnectedness of mankind's set of experiences and the all-inclusive insights that tie us all together.

Moreover, this section fills in as a solicitation for perusers to leave on their own scholarly excursion into the past. As we unwind the secrets of lost civilizations together, we urge perusers to connect with the material, clarify pressing issues, and challenge presumptions. By cultivating a feeling of interest and request, we desire to light an energy for learning and investigation that reaches out a long way past the pages of this book.

In making way for our investigation of lost developments, let us pause to ponder the amazement and miracle of the old world and the getting-through tradition of the people who preceded us. As we venture into the profundities of day's past, may we approach our investigation with lowliness, interest, and a feeling of miracle, for in that lies the genuine quintessence of our common mankind.

2

Chapter 2: Ancient Mesopotamia: The Cradle of Civilization

Ascent of the Sumerians and Akkadians

In the antiquated support of human progress settled between the strong Tigris and Euphrates streams, the narrative of Mesopotamia starts with the ascent of two striking people groups: the Sumerians and the Akkadians. Arising around 4000 BCE in the southern district of Mesopotamia known as Sumer, the Sumerians laid out the world's most memorable metropolitan habitats and laid the groundwork for the advancement of mind-boggling social orders. Their city-states, like Uruk and Ur, prospered in the midst of a scene of fruitful fields, where farming flourished and shipping lanes mismatched the district.

The Sumerians were pioneers in many fields, contributing advancements that would shape the course of mankind's set of experiences. Among their most persevering accomplishments was the creation of composing, known as cuneiform, which reformed correspondence and record-keeping. With dirt tablets engraved with wedge-molded characters, the Sumerians reported everything from regulatory records to writing and verse, abandoning a rich tradition of composed texts that give priceless experiences into their way of life and society.

Close by the Sumerians, the Akkadians arose as a huge power in Mesopotamia, finally laying out the world's most memorable domain under the administration of Sargon the Incomparable around 2300 BCE. The Akkadians, who possessed the northern district of Mesopotamia, took on numerous parts of Sumerian culture and integrated them into their own expanding civilization. Subject to Sargon's authority, the Akkadian Realm extended its impact across the district, joining dissimilar city-states under a unified government and establishing the groundwork for future royal successes.

The ascent of the Sumerians and Akkadians denoted a groundbreaking period in mankind's set of experiences, laying the basis for the improvement of mind-boggling social orders and the rise of metropolitan focuses. Through their developments in horticulture, administration, and culture, these old people groups produced the outline for progress, making way for the ascent of ensuing domains and the blossoming of human imagination and creativity. As we dive further into the chronicles of Mesopotamian history, we uncover the exceptional accomplishments and perseverance through tradition of these spearheading developments, whose commitments keep on reverberating across the centuries.

Accomplishments in Design and Designing

Vital to the wonder of antiquated Mesopotamia were its building wonders and designing accomplishments, which mirrored the resourcefulness and refinement of its human advancement. Mesopotamian city-states, portrayed by their clamoring metropolitan focuses and fantastic designs, took the stand concerning wonderful accomplishments in development and design that left a permanent imprint on the scene and the records of history.

Chief among these design ponders were the ziggurats, transcending terraced structures that filled in as sanctuaries and central places of strict life. Rising gloriously from the level fields of Mesopotamia, these enormous structures typified the otherworldly desires of the old people groups, giving an unmistakable connection between paradise and earth. The most popular of these ziggurats was the Incomparable Ziggurat of Ur, committed to the moon god Nanna, which remained as a demonstration of the power and devotion of the Sumerian civilization.

Notwithstanding strict design, Mesopotamia was famous for its design ability, especially in the domain of water systems. Perceiving the significance of water on the board in supporting horticultural efficiency, Mesopotamian engineers contrived multifaceted frameworks of trenches, dams, and supplies to outfit the waters of the Tigris and Euphrates streams. These water system networks changed the dry scene into a verdant desert spring, empowering the thriving of harvests like wheat, grain, and dates and supporting the development of energetic metropolitan places.

Besides, Mesopotamian design enveloped a different cluster of designs, including royal residences, strongholds, and public structures, each mirroring the exceptional requirements and goals of its occupants. Palatial edifices, like the Imperial Castle of Mari and the Royal Residence of Sargon II at Khorsabad, exhibited the riches and influence of Mesopotamian rulers, while strongholds, for example, the Walls of Babylon, gave security against outside dangers.

The accomplishments of antiquated Mesopotamian design filled reasonable needs as well as typified the social and strict upsides of human advancement. Through their stupendous designs and creative innovations, the old Mesopotamians passed on a getting-through heritage that keeps on motivating wonder and deference right up to the present day. As we wonder about the greatness of their accomplishments, we gain a more profound appreciation for the resourcefulness and vision of the people who constructed the groundwork of civilization in the midst of the ripe fields of Mesopotamia.

Social and strict commitments

Past their structural and designing accomplishments, the old Mesopotamians made significant commitments to human culture and strict ideas, passing on a getting-through inheritance that keeps on forming how we might interpret the world. At the core of Mesopotamian culture was a rich embroidery of folklore, writing, and strict practices that mirrored the mind-boggling convictions and upsides of its kin.

Key to Mesopotamian religion was a pantheon of divine beings and goddesses, each related to explicit parts of nature and human experience. From the preeminent god Enlil, who used control over the breezes and tempests, to the goddess Inanna, who managed love and fruitfulness, Mesopotamian divinities assumed a focal part in the existences of the old people groups, impacting everything from farming and business to fighting and strategy.

The fantasies and legends of Mesopotamia gave structure to grasping the starting points of the universe and humankind's place inside it. Among the most popular of these fantasies was the Epic of Gilgamesh, an awe-inspiring sonnet that relates the undertakings of the incredible ruler Gilgamesh and his mission for everlasting status. Through stories of valor, misfortune, and help from above, the Epic of Gilgamesh offered bits of knowledge about the human condition and the quest for significance in a world loaded with vulnerability.

Notwithstanding writing and folklore, Mesopotamian culture was portrayed by a rich practice of craftsmanship. From unpredictably cut stone reliefs to perfectly improved ceramics and metalwork, Mesopotamian craftsmen delivered works of surprising excellence and complexity. These imaginative manifestations filled both functional and representative needs, embellishing sanctuaries, castles, and burial places and giving a visual articulation of the way of life's strict convictions and cultural qualities.

Besides, Mesopotamian culture was set apart by a feeling of scholarly request and development, as proven by headways in math, cosmology, and medication. Mesopotamian researchers created numerical ideas like the base-60 mathematical framework and the idea of the circle, laying the groundwork for future numerical revelations. Additionally, stargazers took critical steps in noticing divine peculiarities and creating schedules to follow the progression of time.

Through their social and strict commitments, the old Mesopotamians left a permanent imprint on human civilization, impacting resulting societies and forming the course of history. As we dig into the rich embroidery of Mesopotamian culture and thought, we gain a more profound appreciation for the intricacies of old social orders and the perseverance through tradition of their accomplishments.

Decline and vanishing

In spite of its surprising accomplishments and perseverance through heritage, the progress of old Mesopotamia in the long run capitulated to a mix of inner and outside pressures, prompting its downfall and possible vanishing from the chronicles of history. The once-flourishing city-provinces of Mesopotamia steadily fell into decline, their glory blurring as they attempted to battle with a bunch of difficulties.

One of the essential variables contributing to the downfall of Mesopotamian development was the steady danger of fighting and outer attack. Over now is the ideal time. Mesopotamia was every now and again exposed to invasions by adjoining people groups, including the Elamites, Hittites, and Assyrians, who competed for control of its rich grounds and key assets. These struggles, energized by the contest for an area, shipping lanes, and political strength, demanded a weighty cost for Mesopotamian culture, depleting its assets and sabotaging its steadiness.

Notwithstanding outside dangers, Mesopotamia likewise wrestled with inner divisions and political shakiness. As city-states competed for power and impact, competitions and clashes frequently emitted, prompting times of commotion and conflict. Additionally, the ascent of aggressive rulers and administrations, like the Assyrians and Babylonians, brought times of unified rule yet additionally added to the discontinuity and possible breakdown of Mesopotamian development.

Natural factors likewise played a huge part in the decay of Mesopotamia. The locale's reliance on water system farming made it powerless against changes in water accessibility and soil fruitfulness. After some time, escalated water system rehearsals prompted soil salinization and land corruption, decreasing farming efficiency and intensifying food deficiencies. In addition, occasional dry spells and floods, exacerbated by climatic changeability, further weakened Mesopotamian culture, adding to social turmoil and financial decay.

By the first thousand years BCE, the once-strong city-territories of Mesopotamia had been obscured by new abilities and realms, their glory blurred, and their accomplishments eclipsed by the ways of the world. Despite the fact that remnants of Mesopotamian culture and civilization persevered as put-down accounts, engineering ruins, and social practices, the brilliance of long stretches of old Mesopotamia had passed into memory.

Notwithstanding its possible vanishing, the tradition of Mesopotamia persevered, forming the course of mankind's set of experiences and impacting ensuing civic establishments in the locale and then some. From its commitments to composing, science, and administration to its getting-through effect on strict ideas and social appearance, old Mesopotamia made history, helping us to remember the getting-through force of human imagination, creativity, and strength even with difficulty.

The decay and possible vanishing of the once-powerful Mesopotamian developments denoted the conclusion of a significant time period and the start of another part in mankind's set of experiences. Regardless of their wonderful accomplishments and perseverance through heritage, the old city-territories of Mesopotamia confronted various difficulties that at last added to their destruction.

One of the essential variables contributing to the decay of Mesopotamian civic establishments was the unremitting fighting and struggle that tormented the district. The rich fields of Mesopotamia, desired for their rural overflow and vital area, turned into a landmark for contending city-states and domains competing for strength. Ceaseless fighting, combined with interior difficulty and epic showdowns, debilitated the texture of Mesopotamian culture and left it helpless against outer dangers.

Moreover, ecological corruption played a critical role in the downfall of Mesopotamian civilizations. The many-sided water system frameworks that once supported rural efficiency started to vacillate because of disregard, blunder, and soil salinization. Subsequently, crop yields declined, prompting food deficiencies, starvation, and social agitation. Moreover, deforestation and overgrazing exacerbated natural corruption, further undermining the sensitive equilibrium of the biological system.

Political insecurity and interior difficulty likewise contributed to the downfall of Mesopotamian civic establishments. The steady battle for power and impact among rival city-states and traditions prompted times of precariousness and fracture, making it challenging to keep up with incorporated power and a strong administration. Subsequently, the once-extraordinary realms of Mesopotamia started to disentangle, surrendering to inward conflict and outer tensions.

In spite of their downfall, the tradition of Mesopotamia lived on in the chronicles of history, impacting ensuing civilizations and molding the course of human development. The advancements recorded in hard copy, math, and administration spearheaded by the old Mesopotamians laid the groundwork for future improvements in science, innovation, and culture. Also, the social and strict customs of Mesopotamia kept on reverberating through the ages, making a permanent imprint on the convictions and practices of later social orders.

As we consider the downfall and vanishing of Mesopotamian civilizations, we are helped to remember the delicacy of human social orders and the significance of supportable stewardship of the world's assets. The examples gained from the ascent and fall of Mesopotamia act as a wake-up call for people in the future, encouraging us to defy the difficulties of ecological corruption, political precariousness, and social imbalance with shrewdness and premonition. However the once-extraordinary city-provinces of Mesopotamia might have blurred into the ways of the world, their inheritance perseveres as a demonstration of the versatility and resourcefulness of the human soul.

3

Chapter 3: The Mysterious Indus Valley Civilization

Revelation and Unearthing

The story of the Indus Valley Progress, covered in secrecy and interest, started with the fortunate revelation of its old urban communities settled along the banks of the powerful Indus Waterway. In the mid-twentieth century, spearheading archeologists set out on endeavors to the Indian subcontinent, drawn by enticing records of old vestiges and baffling ancient rarities that dissipated across the huge fields of the Punjab and Sindh locales.

Among the most outstanding of these disclosures were the old urban areas of Harappa and Mohenjo-Daro, whose remnants gave the initial look into the wonder of the Indus Valley Development. Unearthing's at these locales uncovered carefully arranged urban communities spread out in a framework design with efficient roads, high-level seepage frameworks, and forcing public designs. The accuracy and refinement of these metropolitan places bewildered the archeological world, testing long-held suppositions about the capacities of antiquated social orders.

As archeologists meticulously uncovered the remainders of the antiquated Indus urban communities, they wrestled with the overwhelming errand of sorting out the riddle of human progress's past. Introductory understandings and speculations about the nature and meaning of the Indus Valley Human progress went from idealistic dreams of a serene, populist society to guesses about a strong, unified state governed by clerics. Be that as it may, as more proof became exposed, researchers started to perceive the intricacy and variety of Indus Valley society, with its complex economy, different populace, and multifaceted social associations.

The revelation and unearthing of the Indus Valley Civilization not only revealed insight into the rich social legacy of the Indian sub-continent, but also opened up new roads of request and investigation into the old past. As we dig further into the records of Indus Valley history, we are helped to remember the extraordinary force of archeological revelation in disentangling the secrets of lost civilizations and enlightening the pathways of mankind's set of experiences.

Metropolitan Preparation and Foundation

At the core of the Indus Valley Civilization lay a demonstration of human resourcefulness and metropolitan arrangement that matched the most progressive civilizations of today. The urban areas of Harappa, Mohenjo-Daro, and various other metropolitan communities dabbed across the prolific fields of the Indus Stream bowl were wonders of old design and association, mirroring a degree of metropolitan complexity unmatched in the old world.

Fundamental to the metropolitan preparation of the Indus urban communities was a fastidiously spread-out lattice example of roads, rear entryways, and lanes, suggestive of present-day city-arranging standards. Roads were adjusted to a north-south and east-west hub, isolating the urban communities into perfectly coordinated blocks and quarters. This painstakingly organized design not only worked with effective development and transportation inside the urban communities, but in addition filled in as a demonstration of the methodical methodology of the human progress' organizers and draftsmen.

Similarly noteworthy was the high-level foundation of the Indus urban areas, which included elaborate seepage frameworks, public showers, and silos. The modern seepage frameworks, made out of inter-connected organizations of underground sewers and covered channels, proficiently oversaw wastewater and tempest spillover, guaranteeing the tidiness and sterilization of the metropolitan climate. Public showers, developed from prepared blocks and furnished with washing stages and evolving rooms, filled in as common get-together spaces for custom filtration and social collaboration.

In addition, the amazing design of the Indus urban areas, including the Incomparable Shower of Mohenjo-Daro and the impressive bastion buildings of Harappa, gave experiences into the strict and regulatory elements of these metropolitan places. The Incomparable Shower, with its enormous focal pool and encompassing rooms, was reasonably filled in as a site for custom washing and purging services, while the stronghold edifices housed managerial structures and world-class homes, representing the concentrated power and social order of Indus Valley society.

The metropolitan preparation and foundation of the Indus Valley Human progress not only worked with the effective working of its urban areas, but in addition mirrored the social and social upsides of its occupants. Through their dominance of metropolitan planning and design, the old Indus individuals made flourishing metropolitan places that filled in as center points of business, culture, and administration, abandoning a heritage that keeps on moving wonderment and esteem right up 'until now.

Exchange Organizations and Financial Framework

Vital to the flourishing and strength of the Indus Valley human advancement was its broad exchange organizations and refined monetary framework, which worked with the trading of merchandise and assets across tremendous distances and supported the metropolitan areas of the progress. Arranged at the junction of shipping lanes interfacing the Indian subcontinent with Focal Asia, the Center East, and then some, the urban areas of the Indus Valley filled in as clamoring business center points, where dealers from different districts met to take part in exchange and trade.

Archeological proof bears witness to the great many wares exchanged by the Indus public, including extravagance merchandise like valuable metals, gemstones, ivory, and materials, as well as ordinary things like ceramics, instruments, and rural items. These merchandise were moved along deep-rooted shipping lanes that crossed riverine and overland courses, connecting the urban communities of the Indus Valley with far-off areas and working with the trading of products and thoughts.

The monetary association of the Indus Valley Development was portrayed as a blend of incorporated power and decentralized creation. While archeological proof proposes the presence of enormous scope for make-creation and specific studios in metropolitan places, for example, stoneware furnaces and metalworking shops, numerous parts of financial movement were probable coordinated at the nearby level, with individual families participating in agribusiness, make-creation, and exchange.

In addition, the Indus Valley Progress's financial flourishing was upheld by its rural efficiency and creative cultivating methods. The rich floodplains of the Indus Stream bowl, fed by yearly storm rains and taken care of by the waterway's occasional floods, gave ideal circumstances to horticulture, considering the development of a different scope of harvests, including wheat, grain, peas, and cotton. The development's dominance of water system procedures, including the development of trenches, wells, and supplies, further upgraded farming efficiency and upheld the development of metropolitan focuses.

Through their broad exchange organizations and complex monetary framework, the old Indus individuals made flourishing progress that prospered for a really long time. The tradition of their monetary accomplishments keeps on resounding in the Indian subcontinent and then some, giving significant bits of knowledge into the elements of old exchange and business and the interconnectedness of human social orders across reality.

Baffling Composing Framework

One of the most persevering secrets of the Indus Valley Progress lies in its baffling composing framework, known as the Indus script. Found engraved on seals, tablets, and different curiosities exhumed from Indus Valley locales, the content has baffled researchers for more than a really long period, opposing endeavors at decipherment and evading conclusive translation.

The Indus script is made out of a progression of pictographic images, each addressing an unmistakable item or idea, organized in direct successions or gathered in groups. Regardless of the endeavors of various researchers and language specialists, the content remains undeciphered, and its exact phonetic and practical importance keeps on evading us.

Researchers have proposed different speculations with respect to the nature and capability of the Indus script. Some recommend that it address a logographic framework, where images compare straightforwardly to words or ideas, while others contend for a syllabic or phonetic understanding, wherein images address sounds or syllables. In any case, the absence of a bilingual engraving or a Rosetta Stone-like curio has blocked progress in unraveling the content, leaving its importance covered in secret.

Intensifying the test of decipherment is the restricted corpus of engravings accessible for review. While a huge number of instances of the Indus script have been found, they are often short and redundant, making it challenging to recognize designs or linguistic designs. Additionally, the shortfall of longer texts or logical signs further convolutes endeavors to unwind the content's importance and reason.

Regardless of these difficulties, researchers keep on investigating new roads of inquiry and utilizing creative systems in their journey to unravel the Indus script. Late headways in computational phonetics, factual examination, and AI have given new devices and procedures to breaking down the content and recognizing possible examples or semantic elements.

While the secret of the Indus script stays perplexing, its review keeps on offering significant bits of knowledge into the social and scholarly accomplishments of the old Indus Valley human advancement. Whether filling in as a type of correspondence, a method for record-keeping, or an image of character and notoriety, the content fills in as a tempting sign of the intricacy and complexity of one of the world's most seasoned civic establishments. As researchers persevere in their endeavors to open its mysteries, the confounding Indus script remains a demonstration of the getting-through charm of the obscure and the unlimited interest of the human soul.

Point 5: Heritage and Effect on Later Human Advancements

The tradition of the Indus Valley Progress stretches out a long way past the boundaries of its old urban communities, making a permanent imprint on the social, social, and monetary scene of the Indian subcontinent and then some. In spite of the perplexing idea of its decay, the development's perseverance through impact should be visible in different parts of later civilizations that arose in the locale.

One of the most important traditions of the Indus Valley Progress is its commitment to metropolitan preparation and foundation. The fastidiously arranged urban areas, high-level waste frameworks, and modern structural procedures spearheaded by the old Indus individuals laid the groundwork for future metropolitan habitats in the Indian subcontinent. The lattice design format of roads and the emphasis on sterilization and general wellbeing set a trend for metropolitan improvement that continued for centuries.

Besides, the monetary framework and exchange networks laid out by the Indus Valley Progress played a significant role in forming the financial scene of the locale. The broad shipping lanes associating the urban communities of the Indus Valley with far-off locales worked with the trading of products, thoughts, and social works, encouraging financial thriving and social trade. The tradition of this exchange organization can in any case be found in the dynamic business sectors and business center points that dab the Indian subcontinent today.

Moreover, the social and strict customs of the Indus Valley Development keep reverberating in the social legacy of South Asia. While the Indus script stays undeciphered, the antiques and archeological remains uncovered at Indus destinations give a glimpse into the rich socially woven artwork of old India. The presence of seals portraying creatures, gods, and ceremonial scenes proposes a perplexing conviction framework and strict practices that might have impacted later strict customs in the district.

Notwithstanding its immediate impact on later developments, the Indus Valley Progress likewise served as a scaffold between the old societies of Mesopotamia and Egypt. The exchange networks that associated the Indus Valley with the civilizations of the Near East worked with the trading of products and thoughts, adding to the dissemination of innovation, workmanship, and social practices across the antiquated world.

As we ponder the tradition of the Indus Valley Development, we are helped to remember the getting-through effect of old civic establishments on the course of mankind's set of experiences. Regardless of the passage of centuries, the accomplishments and developments of the old Indus individuals keep on rousing stunningness and esteem, filling in as a demonstration of the strength, imagination, and resourcefulness of the human soul.

$$4$$

Chapter 4: The Forgotten Empires of Africa

Old African human advancements

In the records of mankind's set of experiences, the African mainland remains a pot of progress, home to a rich embroidery of societies and social orders that have thrived for centuries. From the prolific banks of the Nile Stream to the verdant good countries of East Africa, old African developments have left a permanent imprint on the course of mankind's set of experiences, their accomplishments reverberating through the ages.

Among the most eminent of these civic establishments is Old Egypt, whose fantastic pyramids, transcending sanctuaries, and cryptic burial places keep on enrapturing the creative minds of individuals all over the planet. Arranged along the banks of the Nile Stream, antiquated Egypt arose as one of the world's earliest and most getting through civic establishments, accomplishing noteworthy accomplishments of design, workmanship, and administration that proceeded to stunningness and movement.

Likewise, the Realm of Kush, situated toward the south of Egypt along the Nile Valley, rose to unmistakable quality as a strong domain that equaled its northern neighbor in riches and impact. Prestigious for its talented toxophilites, rich gold stores, and thriving exchange organizations, Kushite civilization assumed a pivotal role in molding the political and social scene of old Africa.

Further south, in the high countries of Ethiopia, the Realm of Axum arose as a key part in the Red Ocean shipping lanes, controlling key ports and overwhelming exchange between Africa, Arabia, and the Mediterranean world. Axumite human progress prospered for quite a long time, abandoning a tradition of great stone monoliths, terrific royal residences, and complicated money that validated its riches and complexity.

Past these notable civic establishments, old Africa was home to a horde of different societies and social orders that made critical commitments to human progress. From the clamoring urban communities of the Swahili Coast to the strong realms of West Africa, including Ghana, Mali, and Songhai, the landmass was a mixture of different people groups and societies, each leaving its own novel engraving on the texture of history.

As we dig into the profundities of old African developments, we uncover an abundance of accomplishments in workmanship, engineering, administration, and exchange that challenge ordinary stories of mankind's set of experiences and feature the lavishness and variety of the African experience. From the perspective of prehistoric studies, grants, and social legacy safeguarding, we gain a more profound appreciation for the getting-through tradition of old Africa, and I

Social and Mechanical Headways

The antiquated civic establishments of Africa were prestigious for their loftiness and power as well as for their social and mechanical accomplishments that established the groundwork for future headways in science, workmanship, and administration. Across the mainland, from the banks of the Nile to the savannas of West Africa, these developments made critical commitments to human information and inventiveness.

One of the most outstanding accomplishments of antiquated African civilizations was the advancement of modern composition frameworks.

In Egypt, pictographs were utilized to record strict texts, authoritative reports, and abstract works, while in the realm of Kush, the Meroitic script was utilized for comparable purposes. These composing frameworks considered the conservation and transmission of information and culture across ages, laying the basis for future advancements recorded in hard copy and education.

Notwithstanding progressions recorded in hard copy, old African civic establishments took huge steps in science, cosmology, and medication. In Egypt, mathematicians created advanced strategies for looking over and designing, empowering the development of great designs like the pyramids. Space experts in Axum and somewhere else noticed heavenly peculiarities and created schedules to follow the progression of time, while healers and doctors in Egypt and Kush rehearsed and progressed clinical procedures and natural cures.

Also, the imaginative accomplishments of antiquated African human advancements are generally celebrated for their excellence, polish, and expressive power. From the dazzling gems of the Nubian sovereigns to the fantastic sculptures of Egyptian pharaohs, workmanship thrived across the mainland, mirroring the social variety and inventiveness of its people groups. Models, paintings, and stoneware were utilized to portray strict subjects, verifiable occasions, and regular daily existence, giving significant bits of knowledge into the convictions, values, and goals of antiquated African social orders.

Through their social and mechanical headways, the antiquated civilizations of Africa persevered through commitments to the worldwide legacy of human development. The tradition of their accomplishments keeps on rousing wonderment and esteem, filling in as a demonstration of the resourcefulness, imagination, and strength of the people groups of Africa all through the ages.

Exchange and Business

Integral to the flourishing and interconnectedness of old African human advancements was the dynamic organization of exchange and trade that spread over the landmass and then some. From the earliest times of mankind's set of experiences, African social orders participated in broad exchange connections, trading merchandise, thoughts, and social practices across huge distances.

One of the main shipping lanes in antiquated Africa was the trans-Saharan exchange organization, which associated the Mediterranean world with the realms and domains of West Africa. Troops of merchants crossed the huge spread of the Sahara Desert, shipping products like gold, salt, ivory, and slaves between North Africa and the Sahelian realms of Ghana, Mali, and Songhai. This shipping lane worked with the trading of important items and cultivated social trade and communication between North Africa and sub-Saharan Africa.

Notwithstanding the trans-Saharan shipping lane, old African civilizations likewise participated in sea exchange across the Indian Sea and the Red Ocean. The port urban areas of the East African coast, like Mogadishu, Mombasa, and Zanzibar, filled in as crucial center points of exchange and business, connecting the African mainland with the exchanging domains of the Indian Sea, including the Roman Realm, the Middle Eastern Promontory, and the human advancements of India and Southeast Asia. This sea exchange network worked with the trading of products like flavors, materials, and valuable metals, advancing the economies and societies of both East Africa and the more extensive Indian Sea world.

The monetary effect of exchange on antiquated African civic establishments was significant, cultivating financial development, social trade, and mechanical advancement. The abundance produced from exchange permitted African rulers to fabricate amazing designs, belittle human expression, and support prospering metropolitan habitats. It likewise worked with the spread of thoughts, religions, and dialects across the mainland, adding to the social variety and dynamism of antiquated African social orders.

Besides, exchange played a vital role in molding the political and social designs of old African civic establishments. It encouraged the ascent of strong exchanging states and realms, like Ghana, Mali, and Axum, which controlled key shipping lanes and amassed incredible riches and impact. These exchanging states filled in as focuses of political power and social trade, drawing in dealers, craftsmen, and researchers from across Africa and then some.

Through their broad exchange organizations and business trades, old African civic establishments manufactured associations that crossed landmasses and hundreds of years, passing on a getting-through heritage that keeps on forming the financial, social, and political scene of Africa and the world. As we unwind the intricacies of old shipping lanes and financial frameworks, we gain a more profound appreciation for the interconnectedness of human social orders and the job of exchange, encouraging success and social trade across existence.

Rise and Fall of Domains

The historical backdrop of antiquated Africa is interspersed by the ascent and fall of strong realms, each transforming the mainland's social, political, and social scene. These realms arose as focuses of force and impact, molding the course of African history and passing on getting through inheritances that keep on resounding right up 'til now.

Among the most prominent of these antiquated African domains was the Realm of Kush, which thrived in the Nile Valley from around 1070 BCE to 350 CE. Arranged toward the south of Egypt, Kush was a considerable opponent to its northern neighbor and assumed a critical role in molding the legislative issues and culture of old Africa. Prestigious for its tactical ability, riches, and social accomplishments, Kush controlled rewarding shipping lanes and set up a good foundation for itself as a provincial influence in the Nile Valley.

Further toward the west, the Realm of Ghana rose to conspicuousness in the district of cutting-edge Mali and Mauritania around the eighth century CE. Through control of the trans-Saharan shipping lanes, Ghana amassed extraordinary riches and impact, becoming known as the "place where there is gold." Its capital city, Koumbi Saleh, was a flourishing focus of business and culture, drawing in dealers and traders from across Africa and the Islamic world.

Following the downfall of Ghana, the Mali Domain arose as the predominant power in West Africa, arriving at its peak under the authority of Mansa Musa in the fourteenth century CE. Prestigious for its immense riches, sweeping domain, and social accomplishments, Mali controlled key shipping lanes and laid out thriving urban areas like Timbuktu, famous for its abundance, grant, and social variety.

In East Africa, the realm of Axum rose to conspicuousness around the first century CE, controlling shipping lanes that connected the Red Ocean with the inside of Africa. Axum's essential area at the junction of Africa, Arabia, and the Mediterranean world permitted it to gather extraordinary riches and impact, turning into a significant focus of exchange, religion, and culture in the locale.

In spite of their power and impact, old African domains were not resistant to the powers of progress and decline. Natural factors like dry season, starvation, and desertification, as well as political commotion, outside intrusions, and the spread of illness, all contributed to the downfall of once-incredible domains.

Nonetheless, the traditions of these old African domains persist in the social legacy of Africa and the more extensive world. Through their accomplishments in workmanship, engineering, administration, and exchange, they laid the groundwork for future advancements in African history and culture, molding the course of human development and motivating generations to come.

Rise and Fall of Domains

The old African mainland saw the ascent and fall of a few strong realms, each leaving a critical engraving on the locale's set of experiences and culture. These domains arose as focuses of political, monetary, and social power, molding the course of African civilization and impacting adjoining locales.

Quite possibly the most conspicuous domain in antiquated Africa was the Realm of Ghana, which prospered between the eighth and eleventh centuries CE. Arranged in the Sahel locale of West Africa, Ghana controlled rewarding shipping lanes that crossed the Sahara Desert, associating the gold-creating areas of West Africa with the business sectors of North Africa and the Mediterranean world. The abundance produced from exchange permitted Ghana to lay out a strong, unified state and support thriving metropolitan communities like Koumbi Saleh, its capital city.

Following the downfall of Ghana, the Mali Realm rose to conspicuousness in the thirteenth century CE under the authority of Sundiata Keita. Mali's abundance and power were based on its control of the gold exchange, which moved from the goldfields of West Africa to the business sectors of North Africa and then some. The domain arrived at its peak under the rule of Mansa Musa, whose amazing journey to Mecca in 1324 CE displayed Mali's abundance and capacity for the world.

In East Africa, the realm of Axum arose as a prevailing power in the Horn of Africa, controlling key shipping lanes that connected the Red Ocean with the inside of Africa. Axum's essential area at the intersection of Africa, Arabia, and the Mediterranean world permitted it to gather incredible riches and impact, empowering it to lay out a strong sea realm that ruled the shipping lanes of the Indian Sea.

Notwithstanding their accomplishments, numerous old African realms in the end surrendered to interior friction, outer tensions, and the powers of history. The downfall of the Mali Realm, for instance, was rushed by inside difficulty, dynastic debates, and the ascent of contending states like Songhai. Also, the decay of Axum can be credited to variables like natural change, political shakiness, and the ascent of Islam, which disturbed customary shipping lanes and debilitated the domain's impact.

In spite of their possible downfall, the traditions of these old African realms persist in the social legacy and authentic memory of the mainland. They act as tokens of Africa's rich and varied history, its commitments to worldwide civilization, and the strength of its people groups even in misfortune.

Current Viewpoints and Rediscovery

In recent years, there has been a developing interest in the review and rediscovery of old African civilizations, driven by a craving to reveal the mainland's rich and various history and challenge Eurocentric stories of the past. Archeologists, students of history, and social legacy specialists have attempted weighty exploration and unearthings to reveal new insight into Africa's old past and protect its social legacy for people in the future.

Endeavors to rediscover antiquated African civilizations have been worked on by propels in archeological procedures, innovation, and interdisciplinary cooperation. Through hands-on work, overviews, and unearthings, archeologists have revealed new archeological destinations, antiquities, and proof of old African civilizations, giving important bits of knowledge into their accomplishments, social practices, and communications with adjoining locales.

Besides, drives to save and safeguard Africa's social legacy have picked up speed as of late, determined by an acknowledgment of the significance of defending the mainland's rich and varied history. UNESCO World Legacy destinations, for example, the pyramids of Egypt, the stone-cut holy places of Lalibela in Ethiopia, and the old city of Extraordinary Zimbabwe, act as demonstrations of Africa's social legacy and draw in guests from around the world.

Notwithstanding archeological examination and social legacy protection, training and public effort assume a critical role in advancing mindfulness and enthusiasm for Africa's old civic establishments. Historical centers, shows, and instructive projects offer open doors for individuals to find out about Africa's rich and different history and draw on its social legacy in significant ways.

As we keep on uncovering the secrets of Africa's old past and rediscovering the accomplishments of its civilizations, we gain a more profound appreciation for the landmass' commitments to human development and the interconnectedness of its people groups with the more extensive world. By observing Africa's social legacy and saving its antiquated human advancements, we honor the strength, imagination, and inventiveness of the people groups of Africa all through the ages.

5

Chapter 5: The Mysteries of Pre-Columbian America

Investigation of Old Civic Establishments

In the archives of mankind's set of experiences, the civic establishments that flourished in pre-Columbian America stand as a demonstration of the resourcefulness, strength, and social lavishness of the native people groups of the Americas. Traversing huge geological areas and enveloping assorted scenes, these old civic establishments left a permanent imprint on the set of experiences and culture of the Americas, forming the course of human improvement in the western half of the globe.

Among the most eminent of these civilizations are the Olmec, Maya, Aztec, and Inca, each of which prospered in various time spans and geological districts, contributing extraordinary social, structural, and mechanical accomplishments to the embroidery of human civilization. The Olmec, known for their titanic stone heads and stylized focuses, established the groundwork for later Mesoamerican civilizations with their advancements in horticulture, exchange, and craftsmanship. The Maya, famous for their stupendous design, many-sided schedule frameworks, and modern composition framework, constructed immense city-states in the wildernesses of present-day Mexico, Guatemala,

Belize, and Honduras. The Aztec, known for their supreme capital of Tenochtitlan and their imposing military ability, manufactured a strong realm in central Mexico that ruled quite a bit of Mesoamerica before the appearance of the Spanish conquerors. Also, the Inca, famous for their amazing stone engineering, broad street organizations, and complicated social associations, fabricated quite possibly the biggest realm in the Americas, extending from present-day Colombia to Chile.

These antiquated developments accomplished surprising accomplishments in designing, creativity, and administration, building fantastic urban areas, sanctuaries, and fortresses that matched the extraordinary civic establishments of the Old World. They created complex rural procedures, for example, terraced cultivating and water system frameworks, that permitted them to support huge populations in assorted and testing conditions. They likewise made huge headways in science, cosmology, and medication, creating complex schedule frameworks, noticing divine peculiarities, and rehearsing carefully developed procedures.

Through their accomplishments, pre-Columbian civilizations in the Americas made commitments to human progress, passing on an enduring heritage that keeps on being praised and contemplated right up 'until now. As we investigate the profundities of their social, compositional, and mechanical accomplishments, we gain a more profound appreciation for the intricacy and variety of human social orders in the Americas and the interconnectedness of societies across existence.

Puzzling Gigantic Designs

One of the most spellbinding parts of pre-Columbian America is the presence of confounding massive designs worked by old civilizations, which continue to interest and perplex researchers and guests alike. These great developments, described by their monstrous size, mind-boggling engineering, and frequently baffling beginnings, act as unmistakable tokens of the creativity and social refinement of the native people groups of the Americas.

Among the most notorious instances of pre-Columbian massive designs are the huge stone tops of the Olmec progress, dispersed across the scene of present-day Mexico. Cut from volcanic basalt rock, these overwhelming models portray cryptic human appearances with particular highlights, bringing up issues about their motivation and importance. A few researchers accept that the stone heads might have filled in as pictures of Olmec rulers or divinities, while others hypothesize about their part in strict customs or political functions.

Notwithstanding the stone tops of the Olmec, pre-Columbian America is likewise home to an abundance of other gigantic designs, including the transcending pyramids of the Maya development, the unpredictable stone sanctuaries of the Inca, and the enormous earthen hills of the Mississippian culture in North America. These designs, worked with striking accuracy and design expertise, filled different needs, going from strict functions and galactic perceptions to political ceremonies and parties.

One of the getting-through secrets encompassing pre-Columbian gigantic designs is the high level of information and methods utilized by old civilizations in their development. Regardless of coming up short on the wheel, draft creatures, or metal apparatuses, native people groups of the Americas had the option to quarry, transport, and erect gigantic stones weighing many tons, frequently over huge spans. The accuracy of their craftsmanship and the intricacy of their building plans keep bewildering archeologists and specialists, rousing continuous examination and hypothesis into the strategies and inspirations driving their development.

Besides, numerous pre-Columbian gigantic designs show exact galactic arrangements and arrangements with regular milestones, proposing a profound comprehension of divine peculiarities and a love for the normal world. The arrangement of sanctuaries and pyramids with the developments of the sun, moon, and stars filled both viable and representative needs, directing strict functions, agrarian exercises, and social customs.

As we wonder about the perplexing massive designs of pre-Columbian America, we are helped to remember the inventiveness, imagination, and social extravagance of the native people groups of the

Americas. These amazing developments stand as persevering demonstrations of the profound, imaginative, and mechanical accomplishments of antiquated civilizations, welcoming us to consider the secrets of the past and examine the interconnectedness of mankind's set of experiences across landmasses and hundreds of years.

Secrets of Lost Urban Communities

Pre-Columbian America is dabbed with the remainders of lost urban areas and archeological locales that keep on spellbinding the creative mind and fueling hypotheses about their starting points and importance. These unwanted metropolitan places, when clamoring as center points of development, hold the keys to opening the mysteries of old societies and civic establishments that prospered in the Americas some time before the appearance of Europeans.

One such confounding site is Teotihuacan, situated in the good countries of central Mexico. Known as the "City of the Divine Beings," Teotihuacan was quite possibly the biggest city in the old world, with a population assessed at north of 100,000 occupants at its pinnacle. The city is portrayed by its stupendous pyramids, sanctuaries, and private edifices, including the Pyramid of the Sun, the Pyramid of the Moon, and the Sanctuary of the Padded Snake. Regardless of its loftiness, the beginnings of Teotihuacan remain covered in secrecy, with researchers discussing its social affiliations, political associations, and possible downfall.

One more unbelievable city of pre-Columbian America is El Dorado, the legendary city of gold said to have been found someplace in the wildernesses of South America. The mission for El Dorado dazzled European voyagers and swashbucklers for a really long time, prompting various endeavors looking for its famous wealth. While El Dorado has never been found, the legend keeps on generating interest and hypotheses about the presence of lost human advancements and secret fortunes in the Amazon rainforest.

In the Andean locale of South America, the secretive remains of Machu Picchu stand as a demonstration of the creativity and engineering ability of the Inca civilization. Roosted high in the Andes mountains, Machu Picchu is eminent for its staggering terraced fields, stone sanctuaries, and imperial homes, which are remembered to have filled in as a retreat for Inca rulers and aristocrats. Regardless of broad exploration and uncovering, many inquiries remain unanswered about the reason and capability of Machu Picchu, powering continuous discussion among archeologists and history specialists.

The investigation of lost urban areas and archeological destinations in pre-Columbian America offers significant bits of knowledge into the ascent and fall of antiquated developments and the intricacies of human social orders in the Americas. Through archeological examination, logical investigation, and interdisciplinary cooperation, researchers keep on disentangling the secrets of these antiquated metropolitan habitats, revealing new insight into the social, political, and financial elements of pre-Columbian America.

As we investigate the remains of lost urban communities and dive into the secrets of pre-Columbian America, we are helped to remember the strength, innovativeness, and social extravagance of the native people groups of the Americas. These antiquated metropolitan habitats act as unmistakable tokens of the getting-through tradition of pre-Columbian civic establishments and the interconnectedness of mankind's set of experiences across existence.

Customs, Convictions, and Cosmology

Fundamental to the otherworldly and social existence of pre-Columbian American human advancements were perplexing customs, complex conviction frameworks, and cosmological perspectives that formed each part of day-to-day existence. These profound practices and convictions gave a system for grasping the normal world, deciphering divine peculiarities, and exploring the intricacies of human life.

Across the assorted scene of pre-Columbian America, native people groups created rich and various strict customs that mirrored their novel social legacy and geological environmental elements. Among the Maya development of Mesoamerica, for instance, strict functions and ceremonies were unpredictably woven into the structure holding the system together, with clerics and shamans filling in as middlemen between the human and heavenly domains. Customs like blood draining, human penance, and stylized ballgames assumed a focal part in regard to divine beings, guaranteeing horticultural richness, and keeping up with grandiose equilibrium.

Additionally, the Aztec human advancement of focal Mexico rehearsed elaborate strict functions and forfeits as a component of their cosmological perspective. The key to Aztec religion was faith in a pantheon of divine beings and goddesses who controlled the powers of nature and human fate. For example, the renowned Templo City chairman penances, in which hostages were proposed to the divine beings in intricate services, were accepted to pacify the divinities and guarantee the continued success of Aztec society.

In the Andean district of South America, the Inca civilization fostered a mind-bogglingly strict framework revolved around the love of nature and hereditary spirits. The Inca had faith in the holiness of the normal world, including mountains, streams, and divine bodies, and rehearsed customs like contributions, functions, and journeys to respect these consecrated substances. The Inca likewise respected their progenitors and embalmed their dead, accepting that the spirits of the departed kept on assuming a part in the issues of the living.

At the core of pre-Columbian strict convictions and practices was a significant love for the normal world and an acknowledgment of humankind's interconnectedness with the universe. Customs, functions, and celebrations served as articulations of commitment and devotion as well as systems for keeping up with social attachment, building up social personality, and deciphering the secrets of the universe.

As we dig into the customs, convictions, and cosmological perspectives of pre-Columbian American civic establishments, we gain a more profound appreciation for the otherworldly extravagance and social variety of native people groups in the Americas. These old strict practices keep on reverberating in contemporary native societies, helping us to remember the perseverance through tradition of pre-Columbian civilizations and the significant associations between people, nature, and the heavenly.

Inheritance and social legacy

The tradition of pre-Columbian American human advancements stretches out a long way past the bounds of old history, forming the social legacy and personality of native people groups in the Americas and impacting contemporary society in significant ways. In spite of the disturbances and changes created by European colonization and the ensuing rushes of globalization, the social tradition of pre-Columbian developments keeps on resounding in the traditions, customs, and imaginative articulations of native networks across the Americas.

One of the most important traditions of pre-Columbian civilizations is their great engineering, which proceeds to stunningness and move guests to archeological destinations like Teotihuacan, Machu Picchu, and Tikal. These old metropolitan habitats act as unmistakable tokens of the structural ability and design creativity of native people groups, protecting their social legacy for people in the future and filling in as images of pride and personality for contemporary native networks.

Moreover, the imaginative accomplishments of pre-Columbian civilizations keep on affecting contemporary native artistic expressions, including painting, figures, winding around, and ceramics. The energetic varieties, mind-boggling designs, and emblematic themes found in pre-Columbian workmanship act as wellsprings of motivation for current native craftsmen, who rework and adjust customary strategies and subjects to communicate their social personalities and declare their presence in the advanced world.

Notwithstanding workmanship and engineering, pre-Columbian civic establishments have left a permanent imprint on the social and phonetic scene of the Americas. Numerous native dialects spoken today follow their foundations in antiquated phonetic families like Maya, Nahuatl, Quechua, and Aymara, safeguarding exceptionally old customs of oral narrating, verse, and tune. Moreover, native cosmologies, fantasies, and legends keep on forming the perspective and otherworldly convictions of contemporary native people groups, giving a feeling of congruity and association with their tribal past.

Besides, the review and enthusiasm for pre-Columbian civic establishments have earned expanding respect in scholastic circles and mainstream society, testing Eurocentric stories of history and hoisting the voices and viewpoints of native researchers and scholarly people. Endeavors to safeguard pre-Columbian archeological destinations, social curiosities, and hallowed locales have likewise picked up speed, driven by an acknowledgment of their significance as storehouses of social legacy and wellsprings of social pride.

As we consider the tradition of pre-Columbian American developments, we are helped to remember the versatility, imagination, and social extravagance of native people groups in the Americas. Their accomplishments keep on moving with wonder and profound respect, filling in as a demonstration of the perseverance through tradition of pre-Columbian civilizations and the strength of native societies despite misfortune. By praising and protecting their social legacy, we honor the commitments of pre-Columbian civilizations to human civilization and reaffirm our obligation to regard and respect the different societies and customs of native people groups in the Americas and then some.

6

—

Chapter 6: Lost Civilizations of Asia

Old Asian Developments

The tremendous and various mainland of Asia brags a rich embroidery of old developments that once flourished across its changed scenes, abandoning a tradition of social, innovative, and design accomplishments that proceed to intrigue and motivate researchers and fans alike. From the fruitful valleys of Mesopotamia to the fog-covered wildernesses of Southeast Asia, antiquated Asian civic establishments thrived in different conditions and molded the course of mankind's set of experiences in significant ways.

Among the most prestigious of these old Asian human advancements is Mesopotamia, frequently alluded to as the "Support of Progress" for its part in the improvement of mind-boggling social orders. Arranged between the Tigris and Euphrates streams in present-day Iraq, Mesopotamia was home to the Sumerians, Akkadians, Babylonians, and Assyrians, among others. These civic establishments recorded critical progressions in math, space science, and administration, laying the groundwork for later developments in the Close to East.

Essentially, the Indus Valley development, situated in present-day Pakistan and northwest India, thrived along the banks of the Indus

39

Stream around 2600–1900 BCE. Known for its all-around arranged urban areas, complex waste frameworks, and high-level metropolitan foundation, the Indus Valley's human progress addresses one of the earliest instances of urbanization in South Asia. In spite of the secrets encompassing its composing framework and possible downfall, the Indus Valley civilization made commitments to the social and mechanical legacy of the Indian subcontinent.

In East Asia, Old China arose as one of the world's earliest and most getting-through civic establishments, with a set of experiences spanning more than 5,000 years. From the incredible Xia administration to the strong Han line, Old China saw the ascent and fall of various traditions, each influencing Chinese culture and society. The accomplishments of antiquated China incorporate the innovation of papermaking, the improvement of Confucian ways of thinking, and the development of the Incomparable Wall, representing the strength and imagination of the Chinese nation from the beginning of time.

Further south, the Khmer Realm prospered in the rich wildernesses of present-day Cambodia between the ninth and fifteenth centuries CE. Known for its great sanctuary edifices, including Angkor Wat and Angkor Thom, the Khmer Domain has accomplished exceptional building and creative accomplishments that keep on astonishing guests right up to the present day. Notwithstanding its possible downfall, the tradition of the Khmer Domain persists in the social legacy of Cambodia and the strength of its kin.

Through the investigation of old Asian civic establishments, we gain significant bits of knowledge into the intricacies of human social orders and the different ways of social turning events. From the fantastic accomplishments of Mesopotamia to the design wonders of Angkor, these developments help us to remember the getting-through tradition of Asia's old past and its relevance in molding the world we occupy today.

Compositional Wonders and Designing Accomplishments

Key to the tradition of lost Asian developments are their building wonders and designing accomplishments, which stand as perseverance through demonstrations of the creativity, craftsmanship, and social refinement of old people groups. From transcending ziggurats and invigorated fortresses to terrific sanctuary edifices and extensive water system frameworks, the design accomplishments of lost Asian developments keep on moving wonderment and adoration, offering looks into the innovative ability and imaginative vision of their makers.

In Mesopotamia, the origin of metropolitan civilization, old modelers and specialists built fantastic designs, for example, ziggurats, which filled in as sanctuaries to the divine beings and central places of strict life. These ventured pyramids, with their terraced levels and forcing presence, represented the power and authority of Mesopotamian rulers and worked with correspondence between the human and heavenly domains. Among the most popular of these ziggurats is the Incomparable Ziggurat of Ur, worked by the Sumerians around 2100 BCE, which remains an image of Mesopotamian human progress right up to the present day.

In the Indus Valley, metropolitan organizers and designers made refined urban areas with cutting-edge waste frameworks, all-around arranged roads, and multi-story structures made of block and stone. The urban communities of Mohenjo-Daro and Harappa, with their network-like formats and proficient foundation, address the absolute earliest instances of metropolitan preparation and design in South Asia. Regardless of the shortfall of stupendous design, the accuracy and productivity of Indus Valley development strategies confirm the high level of mechanical improvement accomplished by the old occupants of the district.

In Old China, engineers and developers built remarkable designs like the Incomparable Wall, an immense guarded fortress extending more than 13,000 miles across northern China. Worked over hundreds of years by progressive lines, the Incomparable Wall represented the solidarity and strength of the Chinese domain and filled in as an imposing hindrance against attacking migrant clans. Moreover, Old China is prestigious for its excellent castles, sanctuaries, and pagodas, which mirror the building and imaginative accomplishments of progressive traditions like the Qin, Han, Tang, and Melody.

In Southeast Asia, the Khmer Realm left an enduring tradition of design magnificence with its radiant sanctuary buildings, most notably Angkor Wat. Implicit in the twelfth century by Ruler Suryavarman II, Angkor Wat is the biggest strict landmark on the planet and a show-stopper of Khmer design. Its transcending towers, many-sided bas-reliefs, and broad canal represent the imaginative and designing abilities of the Khmer people, exhibiting their commitment to strict dedication and social glory.

As we wonder about the design wonders and accomplishments of lost Asian civic establishments, we are helped to remember the groundbreaking force of human imagination and advancement. These amazing designs not only demonstrate the veracity of the accomplishments of old people groups, but in addition act as getting through images of social personality, aggregate memory, and the getting through tradition of Asia's antiquated past.

Social Trade and Exchange Organizations

The interconnectedness of lost Asian civilizations was worked with by broad social trade and thriving exchange networks that connected far-off locales and encouraged the trading of products, thoughts, and social practices. These organizations of trade assumed a significant part in molding the social, monetary, and political scene of old Asia, working with the progression of products, advances, and social developments across immense distances and various scenes.

One of the most renowned shipping lanes in old Asia was the Silk Street, which associated the civic establishments of China, Focal Asia, the Center East, and the Mediterranean world. Extending more than 4,000 miles, the Silk Street filled in as a course for the trading of silk, flavors, valuable metals, and other extravagance merchandise, as well as thoughts, religions, and creative impacts. Along its courses, clamoring parade urban communities like Samarkand, Kashgar, and Dunhuang arose as lively focuses of social trade and monetary movement, where dealers, researchers, and voyagers from various civic establishments blended and exchanged products and information.

Notwithstanding overland shipping lanes like the Silk Street, antiquated Asian developments additionally took part in sea exchange networks that associated waterfront locales and island networks across the Indian Sea and the South China Ocean. Sea shipping lanes, for example, the Sea Silk Street and the Zest Course, worked with the trading of merchandise like flavors, materials, pottery, and valuable metals between China, India, Southeast Asia, and the Bedouin Landmass. These sea networks assumed a fundamental role in the spread of Buddhism, Hinduism, Islam, and other strict social customs across Asia, cultivating social trade and diverse exchange.

Additionally, the trading of merchandise and thoughts along antiquated Asian exchange networks had significant financial, social, and political ramifications for the civic establishments included. It worked with the development of metropolitan focuses, the improvement of particular art enterprises, and the ascent of strong exchanging states and domains. It likewise cultivated social variety, hybridity, and cosmopolitanism as various people groups and societies connected and traded products, dialects, and advancements.

Notwithstanding the difficulties and dangers inborn in significant distance exchange, including banditry, robbery, and political precariousness, antiquated Asian civilizations effectively took part in exchange organizations, perceiving the financial open doors and social advantages of trade. Through the Silk Street, the Sea Silk Street, and other shipping lanes, they produced associations that rose above political limits and social contrasts, adding to the interconnectedness and dynamism of antiquated Asian civilizations.

As we investigate the social trade and exchange organizations of lost Asian developments, we gain a more profound comprehension of the intricacies and interconnectedness of old Asian social orders and the perseverance through tradition of their communications. These organizations of trade worked with monetary thriving and social advancement as well as cultivated diverse figuring out, participation, and shared enhancement, establishing the groundwork for the cosmopolitanism and worldwide interconnectedness that portray Asia and this present reality.

Secrets of Vanishing

The decay and vanishing of once-flourishing Asian developments remain covered in secrecy, with researchers and archeologists wrestling with complex factors that added to their possible downfall. Across the immense scope of Asia, old civic establishments rose and fell, abandoning puzzling remains and unanswered inquiries concerning the powers that molded their destiny.

In Mesopotamia, with the support of civilization, the decay of old city-states like Ur, Babylon, and Nineveh was hastened by a mix of elements, including natural debasement, political flimsiness, and unfamiliar attacks. The district's rich soil, when supported by the yearly surges of the Tigris and Euphrates streams, turned out to be progressively saline because of unreasonable water system work, prompting soil consumption and farming downfall. Moreover, steady fighting and inward difficulty debilitated Mesopotamian city-states, making them helpless against success by unfamiliar powers like the Persians, Assyrians, and Babylonians.

Essentially, in the Indus Valley development, the purposes behind its downfall around 1900 BCE remain a subject of discussion among researchers. Ecological factors, for example, environmental change, floods, and tremors, might have had an impact on weakening the locale, prompting the deserting of metropolitan centers and the dispersal of populations. Also, proof of savagery and fighting suggests that inner turmoil or outer attack might have added to the breakdown of progress, although the specific nature and degree of these struggles remain unsure.

In antiquated China, the decay of lines like the Han, Tang, and Ming was frequently joined by times of political discontinuity, social agitation, and unfamiliar attacks. Monetary factors like overexpansion, financial blunder, and declining rural efficiency additionally contributed to the destruction of dynastic rule. Besides, outer tensions from traveling clans like the Xiongnu, Mongols, and Manchus presented huge difficulties to Chinese solidarity and power, prompting times of disunity and precariousness.

In Southeast Asia, the decay of the Khmer Realm in the fifteenth century CE was encouraged by a blend of elements, including inner turmoil, dynastic battles, and natural corruption. The consumption of normal assets, deforestation, and soil disintegration might have contributed to farming downfalls and food deficiencies, debilitating the realm's capacity to support its tremendous sanctuary buildings and support its developing populace. Moreover, outer tensions from adjoining realms and domains might have additionally exacerbated the Khmer Realm's downfall and inevitable breakdown.

As we wrestle with the secrets of the vanishing of lost Asian civilizations, we are helped to remember the delicacy of human social orders and the complicated interaction of natural, political, and social factors that shape their fates. Through archeological examination, logical investigation, and interdisciplinary joint effort, researchers keep on disentangling the privileged insights of Asia's antiquated past, revealing new insight into the ascent and fall of once-extraordinary human advancements and the getting-through tradition of their accomplishments.

Heritage and social congruity

Notwithstanding the decay and vanishing of old Asian human advancements, their heritage persists in the social legacy and customs of contemporary social orders across Asia. From the remainders of old remnants to the reverberations of past wonders in workmanship, writing, and religion, the social coherence of lost Asian civilizations fills in as a sign of their perseverance through influence on the personality and aggregate memory of Asian people groups.

In Mesopotamia, the tradition of antiquated city-states like Ur, Babylon, and Nineveh lives on in the archeological destinations that dab the scene of present-day Iraq. These vestiges, with their transcending ziggurats, tangled roads, and disintegrating walls, demonstrate the veracity of the accomplishments of Mesopotamian human advancement and act as unmistakable tokens of the locale's rich social legacy. More-over, Mesopotamian commitments to composing, arithmetic, cosmology, and regulation keep on impacting current culture, forming how we might interpret language, science, and administration.

Likewise, in the Indian subcontinent, the tradition of the Indus Valley development lives on in the social practices and customs of contemporary South Asian social orders. In spite of the secretive vanishing of human advancement, components of its social legacy, like metropolitan preparation, craftsmanship, and strict convictions, keep on molding the character and social scene of India and Pakistan. The notorious images of the Indus Valley development, including the popular "Moving Young Lady" puppet and the "Pashupati Seal," remain powerful images of South Asian character and pride.

In China, the tradition of antiquated administrations like the Han, Tang, and Ming is apparent in the country's rich creative and structural legacy, as well as its perseverance through social customs. The Incomparable Wall, the Prohibited City, and the Earthenware Armed Forces stand as demonstrations of the accomplishments of Chinese development and act as images of public pride and character. Furthermore, Confucian ways of thinking, Daoist lessons, and Buddhist convictions keep on having a significant effect on Chinese society and culture, forming virtues, accepted practices, and profound practices.

In Southeast Asia, the tradition of the Khmer Realm lives on in the social legacy of Cambodia and the encompassing district. The lofty sanctuaries of Angkor, with their multifaceted carvings, forcing engineering, and otherworldly importance, remain strong images of Khmer character and pride. Regardless of the decay of the realm, Khmer social customs, including dance, music, and strict ceremonies, keep on prospering in contemporary Cambodian culture, safeguarding the memory of antiquated wonders and respecting the accomplishments of past ages.

As we think about the inheritance and social congruity of lost Asian developments, we are helped to remember the flexibility, inventiveness, and social extravagance of old people groups and the persevering effect of their accomplishments on the world we possess today. Through the conservation and festivity of their social legacy, we honor the commitments of lost Asian civilizations to human civilization and reaffirm our obligation to protect the variety and extravagance of Asia's antiquated past for people in the future.

7

Chapter 7: Legends and Myths: Atlantis and Beyond

Prologue to Legendary Human Advancements

All through the records of mankind's set of experiences, there exists a persevering interest in unbelievable human advancements, covered in secret and fantasy, whose presence has caught the creative minds of researchers, narrators, and swashbucklers alike. Among the most spellbinding of these fantasies is that of Atlantis, an incredible island progress whose story has risen above the general setting to turn into an image of lost brilliance and secret information. However, past Atlantis, a huge number of other legendary terrains and lost mainland's populate the domains of fables and legend, each with its own rich embroidery of stories, convictions, and social importance.

The appeal of these legendary civilizations lies not just in their fantastical stories of cutting-edge innovation, phenomenal riches, and heavenly blessings, but additionally in their representative reverberation as impressions of human yearnings, fears, and dreams. From the idealistic dreams of a brilliant age to the useful examples of pride and ruin, these fantasies offer bits of knowledge into the human mind and the mission for significance and figuring out even with vulnerability and change.

In this part, we leave on an excursion into the domain of legendary developments, starting with an investigation of the unbelievable island of Atlantis and its importance to Western ideas and creative minds. We will dive into the starting points of the Atlantis fantasy, following its foundations in the old Greek way of thinking and folklore, and look at the different translations and speculations encompassing its area, history, and end.

Additionally, we will broaden our degree past Atlantis to investigate other legendary terrains and lost mainland's that populate the scene of world-old stories and legends. From the indented mainland of Lemuria to the puzzling place that is known for Mu and the legendary domain of Hyperborea, these legendary civilizations offer tempting looks into elective narratives and secret universes, testing our thoughts of the real world and moving marvels and interests.

As we set out on this excursion into the domain of legendary developments, we were helped to remember the force of fantasy and narrating to shape how we might interpret the past and enlighten the secrets of the human experience. Through the investigation of these immortal stories, we aim not exclusively to disentangle the privileged insights of lost civilizations but additionally to dig further into the human creative mind and the perseverance of the mission for information, importance, and amazing quality.

The Legend of Atlantis

At the core of the domain of legendary civic establishments lies the perplexing legend of Atlantis, a mythical island development whose story has caught the minds of researchers, students of history, and lovers for a really long time. The story of Atlantis, first related by the old Greek savant Plato in his exchanges "Timaeus" and "Critias," remains quite possibly one of the most persevering and discussed fantasy in Western writing and reasoning.

As per Plato's record, Atlantis was a strong and high-level civilization arranged past the "mainstays of Hercules" (generally related to the

Waterway of Gibraltar) in the Atlantic Sea. Depicted as an idealistic culture favored with rich grounds, bountiful assets, and trend-setting innovation, Atlantis was said to have been established by the god Poseidon's child, Chart Book, and managed by a progression of big-hearted rulers. Its riches and success were matched simply by its moral and profound ideals, making it a reference point for human progress and edification.

In any case, the brilliant time of Atlantis was not to endure. In Plato's story, the Atlanteans became progressively bad and wanton, surrendering to over-the-top pride and pomposity as they continued looking for power and territory. As punishment for their offenses, the divine beings released a disastrous debacle upon Atlantis, sinking the island underneath the waves and dispatching its occupants to a watery grave.

Since Plato's time, the legend of Atlantis has caught the creative minds of researchers, globetrotters, and trick scholars, igniting perpetual hypotheses and discussions about its conceivable presence, area, and destiny. Some have deciphered Atlantis as an exacting verifiable record, setting different hypotheses about its area in the Atlantic Sea or somewhere else, while others view it as a figurative moral story for the ascent and fall of civic establishments or an emblematic portrayal of Plato's philosophical thoughts.

In spite of the absence of substantial proof for the presence of Atlantis, its legend keeps on applying a strong hang on mainstream society, motivating endless works of writing, workmanship, and diversion. From Jules Verne's "20,000 Associations Under the Ocean" to Disney's enlivened film "Atlantis: The Lost Realm," the account of Atlantis has been reconsidered and retold in heap shapes, each adding new layers of translation and hypothesis to the persevering secret of its starting points and importance.

As we dig further into the legend of Atlantis, we are helped to remember the perseverance through the force of fantasy and narrating to catch the human creative mind and enlighten the secrets of the past. Whether Atlantis is at last found to be a verifiable reality or a fabrication of Plato's creative mind, its legend proceeds to pique our interest, welcoming us to contemplate the immortal inquiries of human life and the inflexible walk of time.

Other legendary grounds

Past the incredible domain of Atlantis, a huge number of other legendary grounds and lost landmasses populate the immense spread of world fables and legends, each with its own special stories, convictions, and social importance. From the indented mainland of Lemuria to the lost human progress of Mu and the famous domain of Hyperborea, these legendary terrains catch the creative minds and interests of pioneers, antiquarians, and visionaries alike, offering enticing looks into elective chronicles and secret universes.

One of the most persistent legends of a lost mainland is that of Lemuria, a speculative expanse of land trusted by some to have once existed in the Indian Sea. Proposed in the nineteenth century as a potential clarification for the dispersion of lemurs and other comparative species across Madagascar, India, and Southeast Asia, Lemuria caught the famous creative mind and became inseparable from the possibility of a depressed heaven lost underneath the waves.

Likewise, the legend of Mu, otherwise called "the country of Mu" or "the lost landmass of Mu," arose in the mid-twentieth century as an implied old civilization that originated before known history. As per the defenders of the Mu legend, this exceptional progress thrived in the Pacific Sea prior to being obliterated on a disastrous occasion, abandoning just dissipated remainders and secretive remnants as proof of its presence.

Notwithstanding Lemuria and Mu, the legendary domain of Hyperborea has spellbound the minds of researchers and globetrotters for a really long time. Depicted in old Greek folklore as a place that is known for timeless spring and ceaseless daylight past the North Wind, Hyperborea was accepted to be home to a race of favored humans who resided as one with nature and the divine beings. While the presence of Hyperborea remains simply legendary, its summoning of an unspoiled heaven immaculate by the hardships of mortal presence keeps on reverberating in the human creative mind.

These and other legendary grounds and lost landmasses offer rich feed for investigation and theory, rousing innumerable stories of experience, disclosure, and secret. While their reality might remain covered in vulnerability and fantasy, the perseverance through charm of these unbelievable civic establishments addresses mankind's natural interest and hunger for information, driving us to investigate the limits of the explored parts of the planet and look for answers to the secrets that lie past.

Logical and authentic points of view

In the midst of the charm and interest of legendary terrains and lost human advancements, researchers have tried to isolate truth from fiction, applying thorough techniques for request and examination to disentangle the secrets of the past. While the stories of Atlantis, Lemuria, Mu, and Hyperborea might enamor the creative mind, the mission of understanding requests a cautious assessment of the accessible proof and a basic evaluation of contending hypotheses and translations.

According to a logical point of view, the quest for legendary terrains frequently starts with an investigation of geographical, archeological, and anthropological information to evaluate the possibility of their reality. Topographical investigations of maritime outside layers and mainland racks might reveal insight into the chance of depressed expanses of land or lowered human advancements, while archeological unearthings and overviews can uncover proof of antiquated settlements and social relics that might be associated with unbelievable records.

On account of Atlantis, for instance, researchers have proposed different areas going from the Mediterranean to the Caribbean to Antarctica, each in light of various translations of Plato's works and land proof. Additionally, examinations concerning the presence of Lemuria and Mu have yielded uncertain outcomes, with advocates and doubters introducing clashing contentions in view of land arrangements, phonetic similitudes, and social dissemination designs.

By and large, the investigation of legendary terrains and lost civilizations has been molded by the transaction of writing, archaic exploration, and similar folklore, as researchers look to follow the starting points and development of these fantasies and their importance in various social settings. Near examinations of creation fantasies, flood accounts, and cosmological convictions might uncover normal subjects and themes shared by assorted societies, giving bits of knowledge into the human creative mind and the all-inclusive journey for importance and amazing quality.

In addition, the assessment of old texts, engravings, and oral customs can offer significant hints about the starting points and transmission of legendary stories and the social settings in which they emerged. By contextualizing legendary records inside their verifiable and social milieus, researchers can acquire a more profound comprehension of the social, political, and strict powers that molded the improvement of these accounts and their influence on human social orders.

While logical and authentic points of view may not necessarily, in every case, give conclusive solutions to the secrets of legendary grounds and lost developments, they offer significant apparatuses for knowing truth from fantasy and enlightening the perplexing transaction of creative mind, conviction, and social memory in molding how we might interpret the past. By moving toward these legends with distrust and thoroughness, we honor the journey for information and truth that lies at the core of human requests and reaffirm our obligation to unwind the secrets of the old world.

Inheritance and Understandings

The tradition of legendary terrains and lost civic establishments stretches out a long way past the domain of verifiable request, making a permanent imprint on the social scene of humankind and motivating heaps of translations and reimagining's in writing, craftsmanship, and mainstream society. While the mission for logical truth might stay tricky, the representative meaning of these fantasies as impressions of human goals, fears, and wants perseveres, welcoming us to investigate the profundities of the human mind and the secrets of the universe.

In writing and craftsmanship, the stories of Atlantis, Lemuria, Mu, and Hyperborea have filled in as fruitful ground for imaginative articulation, moving endless works of fiction, verse, and visual workmanship that rethink these legendary terrains and investigate their secret profundities. From the metaphorical utopias of Thomas More's "Ideal World" to the speculative dreams of H.P. Lovecraft's "The Call of Cthulhu," the tradition of legendary civilizations keeps on enamoring the minds of journalists and craftsmen across types and mediums.

In mainstream society, the charm of legendary terrains has been embraced by producers, game designers, and narrators, who have rejuvenated these legends in cinema, in computer games, and through vivid narrating encounters. From Hollywood blockbusters like "Indiana Jones and the Destiny of Atlantis" to video games like "Last Dream" and "Professional Killer's Belief," the tradition of Atlantis and other legendary civic establishments keeps on motivating stunningness and miracles in crowds all over the planet.

Additionally, the representative reverberation of these legends stretches beyond simple amusement, offering significant experiences into the human condition and the ageless mission for importance and greatness. Whether seen as wake-up calls of pride and defeat or as optimistic dreams of a lost, brilliant age, the legends of legendary terrains and lost developments welcome us to consider the secrets of presence and examine our spot in the tremendous embroidery of vast history.

As we think about the inheritance and understandings of legendary developments, we are helped to remember the perseverance through the force of fantasy and narrating to enlighten the human experience and rise above the limits of reality. Whether established in verifiable reality or existing simply in the domain of the creative mind, these legends keep on motivating miracles, interest, and reflection, welcoming us to set out on an excursion of investigation and revelation into the profundities of the human spirit and the secrets of the universe.

8

Chapter 8: Modern Discoveries and Future Prospects

Headways in Archeological Methods

In the steadily developing area of paleo history, the coming of present-day advancements has introduced another time of disclosure, empowering analysts to peer underneath the outer layer of the earth with phenomenal accuracy and exactness. Among the most progressive of these advances are LiDAR (light location and running), ground-entering radar (GPR), and satellite imaging, each offering exceptional abilities for planning, studying, and envisioning archeological destinations and scenes.

LiDAR, specifically, has arisen as a game-changing instrument for archeologists, giving high-goal 3D guides of territory by estimating the distance to objects utilizing laser beats. This innovation permits scientists to enter thick vegetation and uncover stowed-away destroys and old highlights that might be imperceptible to the unaided eye. From lost urban communities covered underneath the wilderness overhang to failed-to-remember settlements darkened by hundreds of years of sedimentation, LiDAR has opened a mother lode of archeological miracles, changing our comprehension of how we might interpret past developments and scenes.

Likewise, ground-infiltrating radar (GPR) has altered archeological study by distinguishing subsurface elements and inconsistencies without the requirement for removal. By producing radar beats into the ground and estimating the reflections from covered designs and curiosities, GPR can make nitty-gritty pictures of archeological destinations and stratigraphy, assisting specialists with recognizing potential exhuming targets and focusing on regions for additional examination. This painless strategy has demonstrated importance for safeguarding delicate locales and limiting aggravation to social legacy while amplifying the proficiency and viability of archaeological hands-on work.

Notwithstanding LiDAR and GPR, satellite imaging has turned into a fundamental device for archeologists, giving high-goal symbolism to archeological locales and scenes from space. By catching multispectral information across various frequencies of light, satellites can uncover unobtrusive varieties in vegetation, soil pieces, and geology that might demonstrate the presence of covered highlights or archeological remaining parts. From old settlements and fortresses to horticultural porches and water system frameworks, satellite symbolism offers an elevated perspective of the past, permitting scientists to investigate immense districts and screen changes in archeological locales over the long haul.

As we bridle the force of current advancements to reveal the mysteries of the past, we are helped to remember the groundbreaking capability of development and disclosure in paleo history. Through LiDAR, ground-entering radar, and satellite imaging, we are acquiring new bits of knowledge about the lives and traditions of old civic establishments, enlightening the secret corners of history, and extending how we might interpret the human experience. As we keep on pushing the limits of archeological investigation, what's to come guarantees much more noteworthy disclosures, energized by the determined quest for information and the soul of revelation.

Submerged Paleo history and Marine Investigation

In recent years, there has been a developing acknowledgment of the significance of submerged paleontology and marine investigation in revealing the secret mysteries of the past. Underneath the waves lie incalculable lowered vestiges, wrecks, and oceanic legacy destinations that offer important experiences into antiquated marine civilizations, exchange organizations, and sea history. As innovation and skill in submerged prehistoric studies have progressed, so too has our capacity to investigate and archive these submerged scenes with remarkable detail and exactness.

Perhaps the main improvement in submerged archaic exploration has been the refinement of remote detecting procedures like side-check sonar, multibeam bathymetry, and sub-base profiling, which permit analysts to plan and envision lowered elements and ancient rarities with high goal and accuracy. These instruments empower archeologists to lead efficient reviews of submerged locales, distinguish likely focuses for removal, and make point-by-point guides and 3D models of lowered scenes, wrecks, and submerged structures.

Additionally, propellers in submerged mechanical technology and remotely operated vehicles (ROVs) have upset the act of submerged paleontology, furnishing analysts with the capacity to investigate and research remote ocean conditions and out-of-reach submerged destinations with remarkable accuracy and control. Furnished with superior-quality cameras, sonar situations, and controller arms, ROVs can catch itemized pictures and gather tests from submerged locales, permitting archeologists to concentrate on curiosities and highlights in situ without upsetting sensitive submerged biological systems.

Lately, submerged archeologists have made momentous revelations in areas ranging from antiquated harbors and submerged urban communities to wrecks and lowered caves. These disclosures have revealed new insight into the sea history of human advancements like the Phoenicians, Greeks, Romans, and Vikings, uncovering the degree of their marine exercises, shipping lanes, and maritime engineering. In addition, submerged paleo history has given bits of knowledge into the impacts of environmental change, ocean level ascent, and ecological corruption on beachfront networks and sea legacy destinations, high-lighting the significance of protecting these submerged fortunes for people in the future.

As we keep on investigating the profundities of the seas and oceans, the eventual fate of submerged archaic exploration holds extraordinary commitment for uncovering new revelations and untold accounts of the past. Through interdisciplinary coordinated effort, mechanical advancement, and dependable stewardship of our submerged social legacy, we can guarantee that the mysteries of the profound are saved and shared for a long time into the future. By improving comprehension, we might interpret the human experience and the interconnectedness of civic establishments across existence.

Hereditary and DNA investigations

In the mission to unwind the secrets of lost civic establishments, hereditary and DNA examination has emerged as an incredible asset for following the starting points and relocations of old populaces and remaking the hereditary history of human social orders. By removing and investigating DNA tests from archeological remains, scientists can access an abundance of data about old populations, including their hereditary lineage, familial connections, and examples of movement and interbreeding.

Progressions in old DNA research have made it conceivable to extricate hereditary material from many sources, including bones, teeth, hair, and, surprisingly, antiquated antiquities like earthenware and materials. Through cautious extraction and investigation strategies, researchers can recuperate antiquated DNA parts from these examples and contrast them with current hereditary information bases to gather tribal connections and populace elements.

One of the main uses of antiquated DNA examination has been in the investigation of human relocations and population developments since the beginning of time. By contrasting the hereditary marks of antiquated people with current populaces, scientists can follow the ways of old movements and reproduce the peopling of landmasses and districts north of millennia. From the peopling of the Americas to the spread of farming in Europe and Asia, antiquated DNA examination has revealed new insight into the complicated transaction of human hereditary qualities, culture, and climate in molding the variety of the human species.

In addition, hereditary examination has given bits of knowledge into the hereditary variety and populace design of old civilizations, uncovering examples of admixture, populace bottlenecks, and hereditary variation in neighborhood conditions. By concentrating on the hereditary cosmetics of old populaces, analysts can acquire experiences into their social association, family relationship frameworks, and connections with adjoining gatherings, improving our comprehension of how we might interpret old social orders and societies.

Lately, advancements in antiquated DNA innovation have opened up new wildernesses in hereditary exploration, permitting researchers to concentrate on old microorganisms, microbiomes, and dietary propensities, as well as the hereditary premise of attributes and sicknesses in old populaces. By joining hereditary information with different lines of proof, for example, archeological, etymological, and verifiable records, scientists can build complete models of human ancient times and disentangle the intricacies of the human story.

As we open the mysteries of the past through hereditary and DNA examination, we are helped to remember the interconnectedness of mankind's set of experiences and the common hereditary legacy that ties us all together. Through interdisciplinary coordinated effort and mechanical advancement, we can keep on pushing the limits of hereditary examination and uncover new bits of knowledge into the starting points and development of old civilizations, enhancing how we might interpret the human excursion across existence.

Environmental Change and Natural Investigations

Lately, the area of paleo history has progressively perceived the basic job of environmental change and natural examinations in forming the directions of past civilizations and understanding the elements that contributed to their ascent and fall. By coordinating archeological proof with palaeoclimatological information, ecological science, and geospatial examination, specialists are acquiring new bits of knowledge into the complicated connection between human social orders and their regular habitats, enlightening the weaknesses and variations of old developments despite natural change.

One of the critical commitments of environmental change examination to paleontology has been the identification of past environmental variances and their effect on human social orders. Through the examination of intermediary pointers, for example, tree rings, ice centers, and residue centers, researchers can reproduce past environments and natural circumstances with exceptional accuracy, permitting archeologists to relate times of ecological change with shifts in human settlement designs, resource methodologies, and social practices. From the breakdown of old civilizations, for example, the Maya and the Akkadian Domain, to the surrender of settlements in the old Near East and the Mediterranean, environmental change played a critical role in molding the course of mankind's set of experiences.

Additionally, ecological examinations have given bits of knowledge into the manners by which human social orders have connected with and changed their regular habitats over the long run. By concentrating on old farming practices, land use examples, and asset management methodologies, specialists can evaluate the maintainability of past developments and distinguish illustrations for contemporary natural difficulties. From the terraced scenes of the Andes to the water system frameworks of Mesopotamia and the deforestation of Easter Island, the natural impression of past civic establishments offers significant insights into the drawn-out results of human movement in the world.

As well as concentrating on the effects of past environmental change and human movement on old developments, ecological exploration is additionally advising our comprehension regarding contemporary natural difficulties and the significance of practical assets. By drawing examples from an earlier time and coordinating conventional information with logical skill, archeologists and ecological researchers are cooperating to foster creative answers for squeezing natural issues, for example, environmental change, biodiversity misfortune, and biological system corruption. Through interdisciplinary coordinated effort and an all-encompassing way to deal with understanding human-climate connections, we can fabricate a stronger and more reasonable future for a long time into the future.

Possibilities for Future Revelations and Exploration

As we stand near the very edge of another time of archeological investigation, the possibilities for future revelations and exploration are more encouraging than any other time in recent memory. With headways in innovation, interdisciplinary coordinated effort, and worldwide participation, archeologists are ready to open new bits of knowledge into the secrets of the past and reveal the secret mysteries of lost civic establishments in the years to come.

One area of potential development is the investigation of unfamiliar districts and remote scenes that have stayed out of reach or underexplored because of calculated difficulties or political imperatives. From the profundities of the Amazon rainforest to the remote corners of the Cold Circle, there are innumerable archeological treasures ready to be found, offering enticing looks into the variety of human societies and narratives across the globe.

Additionally, the advancement of new innovations and logical strategies holds incredible commitment for growing the extension and accuracy of archeological exploration. From propels in remote detecting and geospatial examination to the use of man-made brainpower and AI, these devices are reforming the manner in which we study and decipher archeological information, empowering us to reveal stowed-away examples, connections, and bits of knowledge that were already past our range.

Interdisciplinary cooperation is likewise key to the eventual fate of paleontology, as analysts from different fields meet up to handle complex inquiries and investigate new outskirts of information. By overcoming any barrier between prehistoric studies, humanities, hereditary qualities, natural science, and different disciplines, we can acquire a more complete comprehension of the past and address squeezing difficulties, for example, environmental change, social legacy safeguarding, and native freedoms.

Moreover, the significance of capable stewardship and local area commitment couldn't possibly be more significant in that frame of mind of antiquarianism. As we reveal new revelations and experiences, it is fundamental that we work intimately with neighborhood networks, native people groups, and partners to guarantee that archeological examination is directed morally, deferentially, and in light of our interests, everything being equal. By cultivating a feeling of cooperation and shared regard, we can fabricate trust, encourage exchange, and engage networks to safeguard their social legacy for people in the future.

All in all, the eventual fate of paleontology is splendid, with conceivable outcomes, as we set out on an excursion of revelation and investigation into the profundities of mankind's set of experiences and culture. By embracing development, joint effort, and mindful stewardship, we can keep on opening up the privileged insights of the past and fabricate a more comprehensive and practical future for all.

9

Chapter 9: Conclusion: Learning from the Past

Reflections on Lost Human Advancements

As we arrive at the end of our excursion through the records of history and legend, the time has come to stop and consider the significant experiences acquired from our investigation of lost civic establishments. All through this book, we have dug into the profundities of existence, uncovering the narratives of antiquated domains, evaporated societies, and legendary domains that have caught the creative minds of mankind for centuries.

Our appearance starts with a profound appreciation for the rich embroidery of human experience and creativity that these lost developments address. From the superb remains of old urban communities to the cryptic images of neglected societies, every curio and landmark fills in as a demonstration of the imagination, strength, and yearnings of past social orders. Whether it be the transcending pyramids of Egypt, the rambling urban areas of Mesopotamia, or the perplexing carvings of Mesoamerica, these leftovers of the past address the persevering through tradition of human progress and the getting through journey for significance and amazing quality.

In addition, our process has offered priceless insights into the intricacies of mankind's set of experiences and the horde of factors that shape the ascent and fall of human advancements. From natural changes and mechanical advancements to social disturbances and social trade, we have seen the exchange of powers that push social orders to significance or lead them to destruction. By concentrating on the victories and disappointments of past developments, we gain a more profound comprehension of the difficulties and potential open doors that stand up to us in the current day and the significance of flexibility, versatility, and supportability in building a superior future.

However, our appearance additionally prompts us to defy the sobering real factors of misfortune and annihilation that go with the progression of time. As we wonder about the accomplishments of old societies, we are helped to remember the delicacy of human under-takings and the temporariness of natural realms. The vestiges of lost urban communities and the quietness of evaporated developments act as piercing tokens of the fleetingness of life and the unyielding walk of history, encouraging us to appreciate the gifts of the past and protect the fortunes of our common social legacy for people in the future.

All in all, our appearance at lost developments moves us to embrace the examples of the past, commend the variety of human experience, and develop a feeling of miracle and interest in our general surroundings. As we bid goodbye to the old domains and legendary domains that have spellbound our creative minds, we convey forward the light of information and understanding regarding the tradition of the past while charting a course toward a more splendid and more edified future for all.

Examples Learned

All through our investigation of lost civic establishments, we have gathered important illustrations that resound across existence, offering bits of knowledge into the human condition and the difficulties of exploring the intricacies of the world. As we consider the victories and hardships of old social orders, a few key illustrations arise, each filling in as a directing reference point for contemporary society and people in the future.

One of the chief illustrations learned is the significance of strength even with affliction. Consistently, we have seen how developments have endured storms, overcome obstructions, and miraculously risen like a phoenix after rout to accomplish significance. Whether it be the endurance of the antiquated Egyptians in the midst of the cruel states of the Nile Delta, the flexibility of the Maya even with natural difficulties, or the steadiness of the Romans directly following political disturbance, these accounts of strength help us to remember the unstoppable soul of humankind and the force of diligence notwithstanding misfortune.

Furthermore, our investigation of lost developments highlights the basic significance of transformation and advancement in the endurance and progress of social orders. From the rural developments of the old Sumerians to the designing wonders of the Inca, history is loaded with instances of civilizations that flourished by adjusting to changing conditions and embracing new innovations. By embracing change, encouraging imagination, and developing a feeling of development, social orders can outline a course toward flourishing and progress, even notwithstanding overwhelming difficulties.

Besides, our investigation of lost developments highlights the interconnectedness of human social orders and the significance of participation and coordinated effort in tending to normal difficulties. Whether it be the thriving exchange organizations of the old Silk Street, the social trade of the Mediterranean world, or the discretionary collusions of the old Close to East, history instructs us that participation and shared understanding are fundamental for building versatile and comprehensive social orders that can endure everyday hardship.

In conclusion, our investigation of lost civilizations helps us to remember the delicacy of human undertaking and the basics of stewardship in safeguarding the fortunes of our common social legacy for people in the future. As we take the stand concerning the annihilation of old landmarks, the plundering of archeological destinations, and the disintegration of social practices, we are helped to remember the earnest need to safeguard and save the tradition of the past to support all mankind.

All in all, the illustrations gained from lost civilizations act as a signal of shrewdness and knowledge, directing us on our excursion through the intricacies of the world. By embracing versatility, transformation, collaboration, and stewardship, we can respect the tradition of the past while building a more brilliant and economical future for a long time into the future.

Protecting social legacy

As we finish up our investigation of lost human advancements, we are constrained to consider the significance of saving social legacy and archaeological locales to support present and future generations. The remainders of old civic establishments—their landmarks, curiosities, and social practices—act as windows into the past, offering significant bits of knowledge into the variety of human experience and the accomplishments of our progenitors. However, as we wonder about the miracles of the past, we are likewise defied by the sobering truth of social legacy annihilation and misfortune.

Across the globe, archeological destinations and social legacy are in danger from a bunch of variables, including plundering, defacing, metropolitan turns of events, and cataclysmic events. The looting of archeological destinations for benefit, the annihilation of old landmarks for philosophical reasons, and the disintegration of social customs through disregard and detachment present grave dangers to the conservation of our common legacy. The deficiency of indispensable antiques and landmarks not only denies people in the future their social legacy, but additionally lessens our aggregate comprehension of the past and the lavishness of human variety.

Because of these dangers, purposeful endeavors are in progress to defend social legacy and safeguard archeological locales from harm. State-run administrations, global associations, and nearby networks are cooperating to sanction regulation, lay out safeguarded regions, and execute protection measures to guarantee the drawn-out conservation of social legacies for people in the future. For example, the UNESCO

World Legacy Program, which tries to distinguish, secure, and advance social and regular legacy destinations of exceptional general worth, assumes an essential role in bringing issues to light and preparing support for legacy protection around the world.

Besides, group commitment and partner contribution are fundamental parts of compelling social legacy protection. By including neighborhood networks in dynamic cycles, enabling native people groups to act as overseers of their social legacy, and cultivating a sense of responsibility and pride in social customs, we can guarantee that legacy safeguarding endeavors are economical, comprehensive, and socially delicate. Through training, effort, and promotion, we can impart a feeling of obligation and stewardship in people in the future, moving them to value and safeguard the fortunes of our common social legacy.

All in all, the protection of social legacy isn't just a question of verifiable significance; it is also an ethical goal and an interest from here on out. By defending the tradition of the past, we enhance how we might interpret mankind's set of experiences, commend the variety of human societies, and encourage a feeling of association and having a place across existence. As caretakers of our social legacy, it is our obligation to safeguard and save the fortunes of the past to support all mankind, guaranteeing that the tradition of lost civilizations perseveres for a long time into the future.

Rousing Interest and Marvel

All through our investigation of lost civic establishments, one general subject arises: the perseverance through force of interest and ponder to move investigation, disclosure, and illumination. From the earliest fantasies and legends to the latest archeological undertakings, the mission to uncover the insider facts of the past has enamored the human creative mind and energized the soul of request for centuries.

At the core of this journey lies a well-established interest in our general surroundings and a craving to grasp our spot in the immense embroidery of history and culture. Whether driven by a hunger for information, a feeling of miracle, or an enthusiasm for experience, the quest for archeological secrets and old fortunes has driven wayfarers and researchers to the farthest reaches of the globe, uncovering lost urban communities, translating failed-to-remember dialects, and unwinding the secrets of disappeared developments.

Besides, the investigation of lost developments fills in as a wellspring of motivation and inventiveness, starting the minds of essayists, craftsmen, and producers who look to rejuvenate the marvels of the past through writing, craftsmanship, and diversion. From amazing stories of lost mainland's and legendary terrains to reminiscent depictions of antiquated vestiges and curiosities, the tradition of lost civilizations keeps on rousing stunningness and marveling in crowds all over the planet, welcoming them to set out on their own excursions of investigation and disclosure.

As well as motivating interest and miracles, the investigation of lost civic establishments likewise fills in as a sign of the unfathomable capability of human resourcefulness and the extraordinary force of information. By opening the mysteries of the past, we gain new bits of knowledge into the accomplishments and yearnings of our precursors and the difficulties they faced as they continued looking for endurance and thriving. From the perspective of history, we gain a more profound appreciation for the flexibility, inventiveness, and versatility of the human soul and the limit of people and social orders to overcome difficulty and accomplish significance.

All in all, the investigation of lost civilizations offers a window into the secrets of the past and a door to the miracles of the world. By embracing interest, wonder, and a feeling of investigation, we can uncover the insider facts of lost civilizations and enhance how we might interpret the human experience. As we venture through the domains of history and legend, may we be motivated to proceed with our journey for information, intelligence, and edification and to love the fortunes of the past for a long time into the future.

Planning ahead

As we close our investigation of lost developments, we are confronted with the topic of what lies ahead for the area of antiquarianism and the investigation of mankind's set of experiences. While our excursion through the past has yielded priceless experiences and disclosures, obviously there is still a lot left to reveal and comprehend about the secrets of lost civilizations and the examples they offer for contemporary society.

Planning ahead, perhaps the most squeezing challenge confronting paleo history is the need to adjust the requests of logical requests with the basic of moral stewardship and social awareness. As we keep on investigating archeological destinations and uncovering old relics, it is fundamental that we do so in a way that regards the freedoms and customs of nearby networks, native people groups, and relative populaces. By taking part in significant discourse, coordinated effort, and discussion with partners, we can guarantee that archeological examination is directed morally, capably, and as per the standards of social legacy safeguarding and regard for human poise.

Moreover, the eventual fate of paleo history will be molded by progressions in innovation, interdisciplinary coordinated effort, and worldwide collaboration. From the improvement of new devices and procedures for archeological studying and investigation to the incorporation of information from different disciplines, including hereditary qualities, natural science, and remote detecting, the area of paleontology is ready for phenomenal development and advancement. By saddling the force of innovation and joint effort, we can open new bits of knowledge into the secrets of the past and address squeezing difficulties, for example, environmental change, social legacy safeguarding, and social imbalance.

In addition, the investigation of lost developments offers significant examples for resolving contemporary issues and molding the eventual fate of human culture. From the significance of supportability and versatility despite natural change to the meaning of social variety and inclusivity in encouraging social union and understanding, the tradition of lost civilizations gives an outline for building a more evenhanded, manageable, and caring world.

Taking everything into account, as we bid goodbye to the lost civilizations of the past, we are helped to remember the perseverance of human inventiveness, strength, and innovativeness. By embracing the illustrations of the past, saddling the force of innovation and coordinated effort, and encouraging a feeling of interest, marvel, and sympathy, we can chart a course toward a more brilliant and more illuminated future for all mankind. As overseers of our common social legacy, it is our obligation to safeguard and protect the fortunes of the past for people in the future, guaranteeing that the tradition of lost developments perseveres as an encouraging sign and motivation for a long time into the future.